HEARTS

HEARTS

JUDITH SIMONS

PHOTOGRAPHS BY DEBBIE PATTERSON

LORENZ BOOKS

NEW YORK • LONDON • SYDNEY • BATH

Picture Credits
The American Museum, Bath: pages 8 tr, 10 t;
The Bridgeman Art Library: pages 8 tl, 10 b;
Christie's Colour Library: pages 8 b.

This edition published in 1996 by Lorenz Books
an imprint of Anness Publishing Limited
administrative office: 27 West 20th Street
New York, NY 10011

Lorenz Books are available for bulk purchase for sales
promotion and for premium use. For details write or call
the manager of special sales, LORENZ BOOKS
New York, NY 10011; (212) 807-6739.

Produced by Anness Publishing Limited
1 Boundary Row
London SE1 8HP

ISBN 1 85967 154 3

Publisher: Joanna Lorenz
Project Editor: Judith Simons
Copy Editor: Deborah Savage
Designer: Lilian Lindblom
Photographer: Debbie Patterson
Step photography: Lucy Tizard
Illustrations: Lucinda Ganderton

Printed in Singapore by
Star Standard Industries Pte Ltd

CONTENTS

INTRODUCTION

Of all motifs, the heart shape must be the most universally appealing. Symbolic of love, affection, friendship and even respect, a heart-shaped gift or one bearing a heart decoration conveys a special message. In religious art, the heart symbolizes charity; in contemporary symbolic language, it can simply show allegiance to a town or even a baseball team. Scratched on a tree, it can reveal the secret affection of one teenager for another. But the strongest association for hearts is that of love and romance, and on Valentine's Day, hearts, flowers, and cupids bring relief to the darkest winter's day. For it has been customary for young couples to celebrate courtship in the middle of February since Roman times, when the fertility festival, Lupercalia, was observed. The day is named after Saint Valentine, who lived in the third century AD in Rome and was executed by the Emperor for going against his edict and holding weddings. The Emperor had banned these because, at the time, he wanted young men's energies turned toward soldiering, rather than romance.

Valentine's Day was particularly important in Victorian times when it was not seemly for young couples to spend time alone together and, very often, their feelings for each other had to be conveyed in coded languages. Traditionally, Valentine's cards and gifts come from secret admirers, who use riddles and codes to perhaps hint at their identity. In Victorian times, cards were often accompanied by flowers, each of which held a meaning of its own. The tradition at that time spawned a plethora of prettily decorated hearts, from lavender bags to pin cushions, heart-shaped greetings cards to cushions.

In quilting, a heart indicates a bridal quilt as it was not considered wise to quilt a heart unless the girl was engaged. However, the heart motif is often found on quilts because, traditionally, a girl was expected to complete at least a dozen quilts as part of her dowry.

Top: Valentine's Day has been celebrated, in one form or another, since Roman times. This Victorian Valentine's card is typically decorated with decoupaged cupids.

Above: "Christmas Bride" is a traditional quilting design; American, 18th-century.

The patchwork and appliqué work was carried out by a girl during her teenage years. Because of the expense of the filling and backing, the quilting was left until she became engaged, when all her friends would gather to help her complete the job.

Left: These delightful enamels, by Nelson Dawson, feature stylized heart motifs.

The heart has long had a place in religious symbolism. The basic heart is associated with Saint Theresa of Avila, while the flaming heart usually represents Saint Augustine or the heart of the Savior himself. The heart motif was also a favorite of the Shakers, a strict religious sect that grew up in America in the nineteenth century. They used the heart to symbolize that they gave their hearts to God. When drawn in a hand, it gave life to one of their leader, Mother Lee's, sayings, "Put your hands to work and heart to God."

Above: Here the traditional Shaker symbol of a heart within a hand has been crafted in salt dough.

Left: This unusual heart-shaped tile was made by London Delft.

Above: This carved wooden hanging shelf features cutout heart motifs; Pennsylvania-Dutch, 19th-century.

In complete contrast to the heavily decorated Victorian hearts of the same period, the Shakers used very plain heart shapes. These could have been tiny crossstitch hearts embroidered into the corner of linens, heart-shaped lavender bags made from simple homespun fabrics, heart-shaped baskets, and even cake tins. It was unlikely they used these for themselves, as they viewed most adornment as unnecessary. However, they made a lot of goods for sale in the outside world, and the heart was a popular motif used for decorating these items.

The heart motif has always been a favorite decoration in folk art. Originally, it was used in Europe from the northern latitudes of Scandinavia, and south through Germany, Austria, and Hungary. Clothes were decorated with hearts, furniture was often painted with them, and hearts were cut into wooden doors and shutters. These traditions were taken to the New World by settlers, and the heart became a popular motif here, too.

As a motif for crafts, the heart is incredibly satisfying. It is symmetrical just along the vertical axis, which makes it easy to sketch out. One of the easiest ways to make a heart template is to simply fold a piece of paper in half and draw half a heart out from the fold. Cut out and unfold, and you have a perfect heart. You can even cut the shape straight from the paper with ease. It is best to start by making a heart larger than you'd perhaps wish, as you can then easily adjust its size or shape.

Above: The heart motif can be translated to all manner of objects, including chairs; American, late 18th-century.

Once the template is made, you can use it to cut out fabrics for appliqué; wood, metals or chickenwire for sculpture; even cakes and cookies for celebration baking. You can use it to cut stencils for decorative work, too. You can also buy heart shapes as bases for crafts, such as willow hearts or dried florist's foam hearts for flower work, for example. The shape of a heart can lend it personality. Full, well-rounded ones suggest a sentimental, romantic nature; while longer, thinner ones are more severe. There is no rule that says hearts have to be symmetrical. They can look delightful if the bottom tip swerves to the side, or even if one whole side is larger than the other. Although the classic colors for hearts range from palest pink to deepest crimson, there is no reason why hearts of all colors cannot be used for decoration. They can be delightful in single flat colors, or given a harlequin or checkerboard pattern. Use a single large heart to make a statement, or let a row of tiny ones decorate the hem of a child's dress. This book is

Above: A French tinware cheese strainer, made in a heart shape and decorated with punched holes.

packed full of inspiration for twenty romantic gifts using a variety of skills. Whether you decide to follow the instructions to the letter, or make adaptations to suit your own style, the result will be a delightful, unique gift for you to make and display in your own home or to give with love.

LOVE AND KISSES SOAP DISH

A novel idea to brighten up the bathroom – a soap dish made of ordinary gardening wire, spelling out the message with a heart and crosses (kisses). This couldn't be simpler to do, and it will even keep the soap from making a mess in the bargain! If you wish, the soap dish can be attached to the wall by inserting a screw through the pencil-sized hoop.

YOU WILL NEED

MATERIALS
thick, plastic-coated gardening wire

EQUIPMENT
wire cutters
pencil
pliers

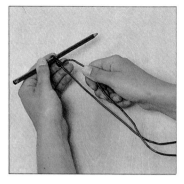

1 Cut a 35 in length of wire and wrap it, at the halfway point, around the pencil. Make a coil, by twisting the pencil a couple of times.

2 Using about 6½ in of wire on each side of the coil, make a heart shape, and then finish off by twisting the wire into a coil again.

3 Using the wire ends left, hook them together and join the ends by crimping them with pliers. Make this loop into an even oval, which will form the rim of the soap dish.

4 Cut four 5½ in lengths of wire. Hook over the outside of the oval, making two crosses. Attach a shorter length across the center.

HEART AND FLOWERS

A heart-shaped dried-flower decoration with a real feel of the country. The construction of the heart couldn't be simpler and it will last a long time, if you don't hang it in direct sunlight. This is a lovely way to preserve the best of summer's harvest of roses.

YOU WILL NEED

MATERIALS
4 long florist's stub wires
florist's tape (optional)
florist's reel wire
hay
dark-green florist's spray paint
clear glue or glue gun
wide, red ribbon
narrow, gold ribbon
large and small dried red roses
dried hydrangea heads

EQUIPMENT
wire cutters
scissors

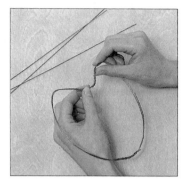

1 Form two pairs of stub wires into a heart shape. The double thickness of the wire gives the arrangement better support. Tape or twist the ends together at the top and bottom.

2 Using reel wire, bind hay all around the heart, to create a firm frame about twice the thickness of a pencil. Work around the heart at least twice with the reel wire, trapping as many loose ends of hay as possible. Cut off and tie the wire, and trim any loose ends of hay. Spray the whole frame dark green and allow to dry.

3 Glue the end of the red ribbon to the bottom of the heart and wrap it around the frame. Repeat with the gold ribbon. Tie a bow at the top with a length of gold ribbon. Cut any stems from the roses and separate the hydrangea into flowerets. Glue the large rose heads near the center and surround them with hydrangea. Put the smaller roses along the top.

HEARTFELT CRADLE QUILT

Reminiscent of American folk art, with its contrasting patchwork squares and heart motifs, this embroidered quilt will look really special in a cradle or crib.

YOU WILL NEED

MATERIALS
54 x 36 in blue cotton
  chambray
6 x 24 in white cotton fabric
stranded embroidery thread:
  white, red and blue
10 x 15 in iron-on fusible
  bonding web
5 different scraps of checked or
  striped cotton shirting
matching sewing thread
24 in square iron-on batting
tacking thread

EQUIPMENT
iron
scissors
graph paper
dressmaker's scissors
dressmaker's carbon paper
pen or hard pencil
needle
soft pencil
straight pins
sewing machine

1 Press the fabric. Cut an 8 in square of graph paper and, using this as a template, cut four squares of blue chambray and five of white cotton. Make sure that you cut all the squares exactly in line with the grain of the fabric.

2 Trace the heart template from the back of the book and use dressmaker's carbon paper to transfer it on to the center of one blue square, using a pen or hard pencil and pressing firmly to achieve a strong line.

3 Using three strands of white embroidery thread, work over all the lines in a small, regular running stitch. Thread the needle with red and work a whipstitch over the inner and outer heart outlines. With blue thread, work whipstitch over the parallel lines inside the heart. Repeat with the three remaining blue squares.

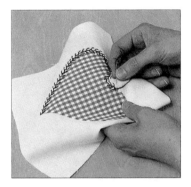

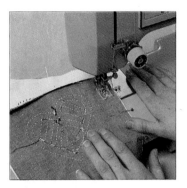

4 Trace just the outline of the heart template on to the paper side of the bonding web. Cut out roughly around the edge and then iron the heart on to a piece of shirting, following the manufacturer's instructions. Make sure that the center line matches the stripes or checks. Cut out carefully around the outline. Repeat with the remaining fabric scraps.

5 Remove the backing paper and iron the heart on to the center of a white square. With three strands of embroidery thread, work a row of feather-stitching around the outside of the heart, to conceal the raw edges. Repeat with the remaining four pieces of shirting and white squares.

6 Lay the nine squares in three rows of three, alternating the colors. Join each row by machine-stitching, with right sides facing, leaving ½ in seam allowances. Press the allowances so that they lie on the blue squares (this prevents them from showing through the white fabric). Pin the rows together, carefully matching the joins. Sew along the long edges, leaving ½ in allowances. Clip the seams where the squares meet and press the seams toward the blue squares.

7 Cut a square of iron-on batting the same size as the completed quilt. Secure it to the back of the quilt, following the manufacturer's instructions. Cut a square of chambray the same size for the backing. Tack it to the back of the batting.

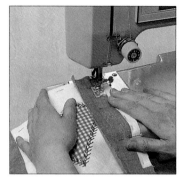

8 From the remainder of the chambray, cut four 2 in wide strips, each measuring 26 in long. Fold them in half lengthwise and press the folds. Press under ¼ in along each long edge. Right sides together, pin in the first strip so that the raw edge lies ½ in from the edge of the quilt. Sew it in place ¾ in from the edge of the quilt. Fold the facing over to the underside, turn in the hem and slip stitch it in place. Repeat for each side, neatening each corner in turn. Remove the tacking.

HAND-PAINTED WOODEN BOX

Decorate a wooden box with simple paint techniques that produce an effect reminiscent of inlaid wood patterns or marquetry, and turn it into a real treasure chest. This technique can apply equally to old or new wooden furniture, picture frames, or even floors, provided that you strip down to bare wood and lighten with wood bleach, if necessary. The skill lies in developing a pleasing pattern.

YOU WILL NEED

MATERIALS
bare wooden box, stripped, and bleached, if necessary
waterproof metallic or glossy paint
2 contrasting wood stains, e.g. brown mahogany and light teak
button polish or clear varnish
wax polish

EQUIPMENT
chalk
pen
small and fine paintbrushes
soft cloths

1 Trace the templates from the back of the book. Enlarge and adapt them to fit your box, as necessary. Cover the backs of the templates with chalk, position them and trace around the outlines firmly with a pen.

2 Soak the paintbrushes, to rid them of loose bristles. Paint on the outlines in metallic or glossy paint and let dry. Fill in the areas between with the wood stains, flooding them up to the outlines. Be careful not to overload the brush. Allow to dry completely.

3 Coat lightly with button polish or wipe on varnish with a soft cloth. Then apply a few coats of wax polish to bring up the sheen and warmth of the wood.

EMBROIDERED BABY SUIT

A ribbon-work decoration for a ready-made romper or sunsuit is easy to achieve and looks really delightful. This type of ribbon work is particularly simple, because you can follow the existing oversewn garment seams, which act as sewing lines. Choose a plain, not patterned, suit, without any motifs.

YOU WILL NEED

MATERIALS
romper or sunsuit
6 yd chocolate brown ⅛ in wide ribbon
3 yd rust ⅛ in wide ribbon
3 yd salmon or peach ⅛ in wide ribbon
chocolate brown and orange thread

EQUIPMENT
needle
soft pencil or vanishing fabric marker (optional)
scissors

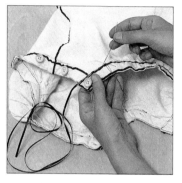

1 Use running stitch to attach chocolate brown ribbon to the seams of the suit. Turn under, and neatly finish ⅛ in at the ends.

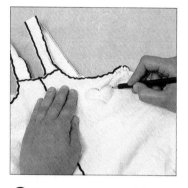

2 Trace the heart motif from the back of the book and adapt the size. Transfer to the suit four times. As an alternative, draw your own motifs with a pencil or marker.

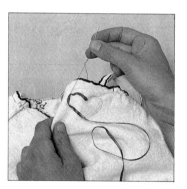

3 Turn under the end of the rust ribbon. Working counterclockwise from the top of the heart, sew in place with running stitch in orange thread.

4 Repeat with the salmon or peach ribbon, using chocolate brown or orange thread.

LOVE-HEARTS WALL PLAQUE

Although the decorative motifs – hearts and farmyard animals – call to mind folk art, the strong pastel colors used to paint this plaque give a more contemporary feel. It would be at home in a light, modern interior.

YOU WILL NEED

MATERIALS
galvanized wire, e.g. from
  coathanger
5 x 5 in cardboard
masking tape
newspaper
wallpaper paste
white latex or poster paint
self-hardening clay
acrylic or poster paints: pink,
  mauve, blue, green, and yellow
clear varnish

EQUIPMENT
scissors
medium and small paintbrushes
paint-mixing containers
modeling tools

1 Shape a hook from the wire. Tape it on to the back of the cardboard with a piece of masking tape.

2 Tear the newspaper into small strips. Dip them in paste and cover both sides of the cardboard with a layer of newspaper.

3 Prime both sides of the plaque with white paint and let dry. Using modeling tools, mold decorative borders, heart shapes, and a central chicken motif in the self-hardening clay. Allow to dry.

4 Decorate with the paints and allow to dry. Finish with a coat of varnish.

WINGED HEART

Τhis salt-dough wall decoration is a charming way to tell someone absent that you are thinking of them – with a heart that has, literally, taken wing.

YOU WILL NEED

FOR THE SALT DOUGH
1 cup table salt
2 cups flour
1 cup water

MATERIALS
aluminum foil
2 screw eyes
acrylic paints: red, white, black, green, blue, and gold
clear varnish
length of cord

EQUIPMENT
mixing bowl
spoon
airtight container
baking parchment
rolling pin
kitchen knife
modeling tools
small natural sponge
paint-mixing container
small and fine paintbrushes

1 To make the salt dough, put the salt, flour, and half the water in a bowl. Mix them together, gradually adding the rest of the water, until the dough has a smooth consistency. If it becomes too sticky, mix in more flour. If it is too hard, add more water. Turn on to a floured surface and knead for 10 minutes and then allow to rest in an airtight container for 30 minutes.

2 Trace the template from the back of the book. Transfer the main outlines of the template on to baking parchment and cut the template out. Roll about two thirds of the dough on to a sheet of baking parchment so that it is about ⅛ in thick. Put the template on the dough and cut around it with a sharp kitchen knife. Make a thin roll of dough to fit each side of the background. Moisten the edges and put the rolls in place. Smooth the joints with a modeling tool and finish by molding a small dough heart for each corner.

3 Using the template as a guide, mold a solid heart shape from foil. Roll out half the remaining dough to a ¼ in thickness and place it over the foil heart. Trim the edges and place the heart in the center of the background. Smooth with a damp sponge. Roll out the remaining dough evenly to ¼ in thickness. Cut out the wing templates from the baking parchment and place them on the dough. Cut around the edges with a modeling tool and make the feather divisions with a modeling tool. Moisten the backs and put them on the background. Smooth the edges.

4 Bake the heart in the oven at 120°F for 2 hours and then remove it and carefully insert the screw eyes on the back, one at each side. Return to the oven for at least 6 hours, or until it is completely hard. Allow to cool. Paint the heart red, the wings white and background black. Following the template and finished picture, decorate the heart with a painted daisy chain and add feathery markings to the wings. Highlight with gold paint and then finish with at least two coats of varnish, to protect the dough. When dry, thread the cord through the screw eyes, so you can hang it on the wall.

COOKIE HEARTS AND HANDS

These are delicious cookies that will most likely be wolfed down as soon as they are cool enough to eat. If you can save them from the ravening hordes, you can turn them into charming folk-art-style decorations, using any scraps of fabric, ribbon, and buttons that you have on hand. They make wonderful homemade Christmas tree decorations.

YOU WILL NEED

FOR THE COOKIES
12 oz flour
1 tsp ground cinnamon
1 tsp ground ginger
½ tsp ground allspice
2 oz soft brown sugar
3 tbsp golden syrup
3 tbsp molasses
2 oz butter, softened
½ tsp baking soda
1 tbsp warm water
large egg, beaten
royal icing

MATERIALS
garden twine
homespun cotton checked fabric
clear glue or glue gun
cotton gingham fabric
buttons
ribbons
picture-hanging hook
cardboard

EQUIPMENT
mixing bowls
sifter
wooden spoon
rolling pin
pastry board
selection of heart- and
  hand-shaped cookie cutters
baking sheet
baking parchment
skewer or bradawl
pastry bag
fine icing nozzle
scissors

1 To make the dough, sift the flour and spices into a bowl. Beat the sugar, syrup, molasses and butter together. Mix the baking soda and water, and add to the liquid mixture. Add the beaten egg, and mix well. Add the flour mixture, a little at a time, and mix until you have a firm dough. Knead gently and allow to rest for 30 minutes. Preheat the oven to 350°F. Roll out the dough thinly and evenly on a floured board.

2 Cut out the shapes and bake on a baking sheet lined with parchment for 10–15 minutes. Make a hole for hanging the cookies while warm, then allow to cool completely.

3 For edible cookies, decorate the cookies with white royal icing, using a pastry bag and a fine icing nozzle.

4 If the cookies are not going to be eaten, put them back in a low oven for a couple of hours to dry them out, so they keep longer. String some together with garden twine. Make bows for tying from checked fabric for some; cut out heart motifs and glue them on others. Do the same with the gingham (which you could dye in tea, to age and tone down the color, if you like). Decorate the ties with buttons and ribbons. Use the bradawl to decorate the cookies with a pattern of holes (or do this with a skewer before baking). Take care not to use too much force or the cookie might break, though you can usually repair the damage invisibly with glue. To make a cookie for hanging on the wall, glue a picture-hanging hook on the back. Large cookies need careful handling. You can glue pieces of cardboard on to the backs, to reinforce them.

HEART-SHAPED WOODEN DISH

This simple, wooden dish would be good for serving candies or nuts. It does require some simple woodworking skills but is very easy to make, if you take the time to measure, draw, and cut accurately.

YOU WILL NEED

MATERIALS
³⁄₁₆ in birch-faced plywood sheet
1 in pine slat
wood filler (if necessary)
wood glue
white undercoat paint
acrylic paints: red, green, yellow, white, and brown
matte varnish

EQUIPMENT
double-sided tape
pencil
fretsaw or coping saw
ruler
drill with medium bit
medium- and fine-grade sandpaper
paintbrushes
paint-mixing containers

1 Attach the plywood to the back of the pine with the double-sided tape. Trace the template from the back of the book, enlarging it as necessary. Place the template on the pine and draw around it. Cut out the heart shape from the plywood and pine with the saw.

2 Detach the plywood heart. On the pine heart, mark a line ¼ in from the edge (make a smaller template and draw around it). Drill a hole for the saw blade. If you can't do this easily, saw through from the side and repair the cut with a little filler. Cut around the inner outline and detach the smaller heart. Sand the two pieces smooth.

3 Line up the plywood heart exactly with the pine one, as a base. Glue it in place and allow to dry. Sand around the edges again. Paint with white undercoat and let dry. Lightly sand again, with fine-grade sandpaper, and decorate with acrylic paints. When dry, finish with a coat of varnish.

SHAKER-STYLE TOWEL

Crossstitched hearts and initials conjure up the art of the Shakers, for whom the heart was a well-loved decorative image. Hearts denoted not the traditions of romantic love, but the spiritual devotion of the movement's followers, summed up in the saying "Hands to work, hearts to God."

YOU WILL NEED

MATERIALS
8 x 36 in homespun cotton gingham fabric
cotton seersucker guest towel
contrasting tacking thread
stranded embroidery thread:
   dark crimson, dark turquoise, and light crimson
matching sewing thread

EQUIPMENT
tape measure
dressmaker's scissors
needle
embroidery hoop
iron
straight pins
sewing machine (optional)

1 Wash the gingham and towel, to check for shrinkage. Cut the gingham 2 in wider than the towel. Mark the center with two intersecting lines of tacking. Stretch the fabric in a hoop. Using the charts at the back of the book, embroider four initials in three strands of dark-crimson thread. Work the second diagonal in the same direction each time.

2 Again, following the charts, embroider the four dark-turquoise hearts in crossstitch on each side of the monogram. Then work the light-crimson hearts. These are given extra definition with an outline of running stitch, worked in dark crimson.

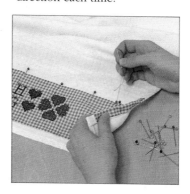

3 Press the embroidery lightly. Trim the long edges so that there is 1½ in of fabric on each side of the embroidery and press under ½ in along each side. Fold the towel in half to find the center point, and pin the gingham along the bottom edge. Turn the sides of the gingham to the back of the towel and tack in place. Then stitch with matching thread.

DECOUPAGED VALENTINE'S BOX

A romantic gift for Valentine's Day, or any time of year. The combination of cut-out flowers and gold hearts gives a really strong, graphic impression, quite different from the usual whimsical "Victoriana" look. Decoupage is an easy technique that gives spectacular results, making it possible to cover relatively large areas with a repeating pattern.

YOU WILL NEED

MATERIALS
plain wooden box
red latex paint
floral wrapping paper
gold paper
glue
antique oak varnish
polyurethane varnish

EQUIPMENT
medium paintbrushes
scissors
pencil
cloth

1 Paint the box red inside and out. Cut out flower images of various sizes from the paper. Trace the template from the back of the book and enlarge, if necessary. Place the template on the gold paper and draw around it. Repeat eight times and cut out the gold hearts.

2 Arrange the hearts on the box, two on the lid and on each long side and one on each end. Glue them in place. Position the flowers around the hearts and glue them, pushing out any air bubbles. Allow to dry completely.

3 Add a coat of antique varnish, and rub it off with a cloth, to give an old, soft look. Then finish with three or four coats of polyurethane varnish, letting each dry before adding the next.

ROMANTIC GIFT WRAP

What better way to present the perfect Valentine's Day gift than wrapped in this hand-stenciled paper with bold hearts? This is an easy stencil to cut out and use. Your finishing touch won't take you long to complete and you can be sure of a professional-looking result.

YOU WILL NEED

MATERIALS
crêpe paper
acrylic paints: burnt umber and gold

EQUIPMENT
acetate sheet
indelible black marker pen
craft knife
self-healing cutting mat
stencil brush
paint-mixing container

1 Trace and enlarge the heart template from the back of the book, and transfer the design on to the acetate sheet with the indelible black marker pen. Cut out the design carefully with the knife, using a cutting mat to protect the surface.

2 Stencil burnt umber hearts randomly across the paper. Allow to dry.

3 Stencil gold hearts on top and slightly to the right. The finished effect should be that the umber hearts look like the shadows of the gold hearts.

KING OF HEARTS MIRROR

This clay mirror frame is very easy to make but looks sophisticated. The heart-shaped, cut-away section, outlined with glittering copper wire, makes a really unusual mirror that will be as welcome for its decorativeness as for its usefulness.

YOU WILL NEED

MATERIALS
copper wire
rectangular mirror
self-hardening clay
turquoise acrylic paint
gold powder
clear varnish

EQUIPMENT
wire cutters
round-nosed pliers
plastic sheet
rolling pin
modeling tools
small paintbrushes
paint-mixing container

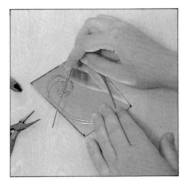

1 Shape a length of wire into a heart shape with an internal curl to fit within the mirror.

2 Shape two lengths of wire into curls with a right angle at the other end.

3 Roll out the clay to a ³⁄₁₆ in thickness on a plastic sheet. Trace the template from the back of the book and cut out a clay "crown," with a wet modeling tool. Cut out a clay rectangle at least ¾ in larger than the mirror.

4 Sandwich the mirror between the "crown" and the rectangle. Smooth the clay to get an impression of the mirror. Lift off the rectangle and cut ½ in larger than the impression. Replace on the mirror, matching the impression to the mirror outline.

▶

5 With a wet modeling tool, seal the join between the two clay layers.

6 Place the wire heart on top and, with a wet modeling tool, cut around the inside of the heart, revealing the mirror. Insert the wire curls on one side.

7 Mold more clay into "buttons," stick them on to the mirror frame under the crown and allow to dry for 2–3 days.

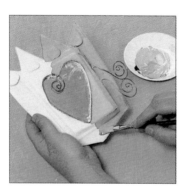

8 Give the clay a coat of turquoise paint and allow to dry.

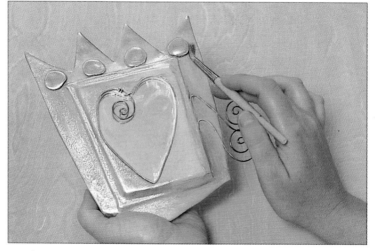

9 With a dry brush, cover the frame lightly with gold powder. Finally, give the frame a coat of varnish.

HEARTS ON THE WING MOBILE

This colorful mobile is made from papier-mâché, elaborately painted with gouache colors. The more individual you make the decoration, the more charming it becomes.

YOU WILL NEED

MATERIALS
newspaper
masking tape
corrugated cardboard
wallpaper paste
screw eyes
epoxy glue
chemical metal filler (car-body repair filler)
mirror fragments
white glue
white acrylic primer
selection of gouache paints
glossy varnish
gold enamel paint
galvanized wire
jewelry jump rings

EQUIPMENT
scissors
craft knife
small and fine paintbrushes
paint-mixing container
wire cutters
round-nosed pliers

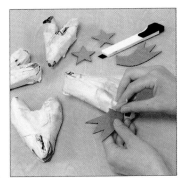

1 Roll up sheets of newspaper, bend them in the center and then bend the ends over, to make a heart shape. Secure the ends with masking tape. Trace the template for the wings and stars from the back of the book and cut them out from the corrugated cardboard. Cut two slits in the side of the biggest heart, slot in the wings, and secure them with tape.

2 Tear more newspaper into strips. Cover all the hearts and stars with several layers of newspaper strips, dipped in wallpaper paste. Allow to dry.

3 Screw small screw eyes in place, securing them with epoxy glue. Allow to dry. Then mix up the filler, according to the manufacturer's instructions. Spread filler on the wings and carefully push in pieces of broken mirror. Allow to dry. Repeat the process on the back of the wings.

4 Coat all the shapes (except the wings) in white glue and allow to dry. Paint on a layer of white acrylic primer, being extra careful and using a fine brush to fill between the pieces of mirror.

5 Paint on the design, using gouache paints.

6 Coat with several layers of glossy varnish. When dry, add detail in gold enamel.

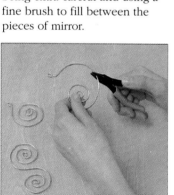

7 Using wire cutters, cut a 16 in length of wire and two 11 in lengths. Using the round-nosed pliers, coil the wire into shape, following the outlines given with the templates at the back of the book. Coat in turn with white glue, primer, and gold enamel, allowing each coat to dry before applying the next.

8 Assemble the mobile using small jump rings and round-nosed pliers.

FOLK-ART PICTURE FRAMES

These simple, graphic frames combine the naïve, hand-painted feel and typical colors of folk-art decoration with a boldness that makes them fit for the most sophisticated modern interior.

YOU WILL NEED

MATERIALS
plain, flat-faced wooden frames
acrylic paints: white, yellow,
* black, raw umber, blue,*
* and red*
satin polyurethane varnish

EQUIPMENT
fine-grade sandpaper
cloth
masking tape
wide, flat-bristled and fine
* paintbrushes*
paint-mixing container
soft pencil

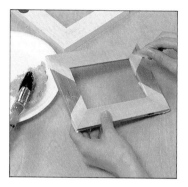

1 Sand the frames to remove any lacquer and provide a tooth for the paint. Wipe off any dust with a damp cloth. Starting with the two long sides, mask off the corners of the frames diagonally with tape to prevent any brush marks from over-lapping and lying in the wrong direction. Mix up an "antique" yellow from white and yellow paint, with a touch of black and raw umber. Paint on the back-ground color on the top and bottom edges; this can be either a single, quite thick coat, sever-al coats, or simply a color-wash, so that the wood grain shows through. Remove the tape when dry, mask the painted edges at the corners and paint the sides of the frames.

2 Trace the templates from the back of the book and enlarge them, if necessary. Paint the templates to try out different color combinations if you wish. Position the templates on the frames and draw around them with a soft pencil.

3 Paint the design directly on to the frames, adding the circle and star motifs. Varnish the frames.

LOVE BUG

A most lovable insect, with a heart-shaped body, perfect for giving as a token of your affection.

YOU WILL NEED

MATERIALS
copper wire
thin copper sheet
self-hardening clay
red acrylic paint
clear varnish
gold varnish

EQUIPMENT
round-nosed pliers
tin snips
rolling pin
plastic sheet
modeling tools
small paintbrushes
paint-mixing container

1 Curl the wire. Trace the heart and wings templates from the back of the book. Trace two wings on to the copper sheet and cut out with tin snips. Roll out the clay on the plastic sheet. Cut out a heart with a wet modeling tool. Model the face.

2 Stick the wings and wire curl into the clay and allow to dry for 2–3 days.

3 Paint the love bug red and allow to dry. Then give it a coat of varnish.

4 With a dry brush, apply gold powder mixed with a little varnish, to finish.

BRIDAL HEART

Pink satin and lace are
the essence of femininity;
this delicate bridal favor
would be the perfect gift of
love on the wedding day of a
daughter, sister, or friend. The
decoration of sequins, pearls,
and motifs can be as simple
or elaborate as you like, and
no two of these will ever be
the same.

YOU WILL NEED

MATERIALS
16 x 8 in pink satin fabric
8 in square lace fabric or
  lace mat
contrasting tacking thread
ready-made silk flowers
  (optional)
matching sewing thread
⅛ in flat sequins
seed pearls
polyester batting
24 in narrow lace edging
short lengths ⅛ in satin ribbon
  in complementary colors

EQUIPMENT
dressmaker's scissors
straight pins
very fine needle
sewing machine (optional)

1 Trace the heart template
from the back of the book
and enlarge it, if necessary. Cut
out two hearts from pink satin.
Place one under the lace fabric
or mat, and move it about to
find the most attractive pattern
area. Pin and then tack through
both layers. Cut the lace, carefully following the outline of the
satin heart.

2 From the remaining lace, cut
flowers and motifs. Sew to
the center of the lace heart. (Or
use silk flowers.) Add sequins
and pearls. Pin the hearts
together, right sides facing. Stitch
½ in in from the edges, leaving a
2 in gap. Trim seams and clip
curves. Turn right side out. Fill
the heart with batting and slip
stitch the gap.

3 Run a gathering thread
along the straight edge of
the lace edging and pin one
end to the top of the heart.
Adjusting the gathers evenly,
continue to pin the lace around
the outside edge and then slip
stitch it firmly in place with
small, invisible stitches. Remove
the gathering thread. Finish by
adding a hanging loop, small
ribbon bows, and additional
beads and sequins.

METALLIC EMBROIDERED JEWELRY

Glittering machine-embroidery, iridescent paper, and shimmering beads combine to make this very special jewelry.

YOU WILL NEED

MATERIALS
water-soluble fabric
iridescent paper
metallic sewing threads
self-hardening clay
blue-green watercolor inks
metallic paints
spray varnish
selection of small beads
2 jewelry split rings
2 earring wires or posts
2 jewelry jump rings

EQUIPMENT
embroidery hoop
straight pins
vanishing fabric marker
sewing machine
scissors
iron
paper towels
stiff wire
paintbrush
cardboard
felt
plastic sheet
beading needle
flat-nosed pliers

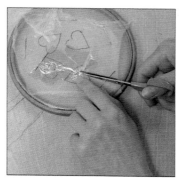

1 Stretch a layer of the fabric in the hoop and pin another layer to the back. Trace the motifs from the back of the book and enlarge them, if necessary. Trace them on to the fabric with the vanishing marker. For the centers of the motifs, pin iridescent paper to the back of the fabric. Thread the machine with metallic thread and experiment with sewing without a foot, with different thicknesses of thread, to achieve the right tension. Consult your instruction booklet for more help. Machine around the heart centers and cut away any excess iridescent paper from the back.

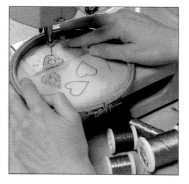

2 Machine around the outline, first in straight stitch and then in zigzag stitch. Go over the design several times, so it is quite stiff.

3 Dissolve the fabric in water according to the manufacturer's instructions. Iron dry between paper towels.

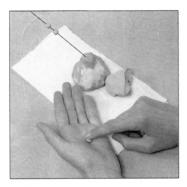

4 Make small balls of self-hardening clay for the beads, and push them on to a stiff wire. Allow to dry, stuck into a piece of clay.

5 Paint the beads with watercolor inks. When dry, add dots of metallic paint, to highlight them.

6 Cover the piece of cardboard with felt and plastic, to make a soft backing sheet. Pin the motifs to the sheet and spray the clay beads and motifs with the varnish.

7 Using a beading needle and metallic thread, attach the thread to the top of the earring. Thread on two small beads, then a clay bead, and two or so small beads. Take the thread through a split ring and then back down again through the beads and into the motif. Fasten off. Sew small beads on to the centers of the motifs, in a ring.

8 To join the earring fixings, open up a jump ring with pliers and thread through the split ring. Join it to the ring on the earring. For a pendant, thread a machine-embroidered chain through the slip ring.

CRAFT TIP

You need a sewing machine that can be used without a foot for free embroidery (most can). Sewing through the iridescent paper does blunt needles, so have some spares ready. You can buy water-soluble fabric from good craft shops.

HEART-SHAPED TRIVET

A practical accessory that would be particularly appropriate in a Shaker-style kitchen, because hearts were one of the Shakers' favorite decorative motifs. The galvanized wire will coordinate with and complement stainless steel kitchen utensils and saucepans.

YOU WILL NEED

MATERIALS
0.078 in galvanized wire

EQUIPMENT
pliers
broom handle

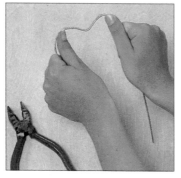

1 Take a 20 in length of wire. Using pliers, make a heart shape by bending the wire in the center, to form the dip in the top of the heart. At the ends, make hooks to join the wires together.

2 Make a coil by tightly and evenly wrapping more wire around a broom handle 50 times. Make hooks in the ends the same way as before.

3 Thread the coil over the heart. Connect the ends of the heart by crimping the hooked ends together with pliers. You will need to manipulate the coil to make it sit evenly around the heart shape, before joining and crimping the ends together with pliers.

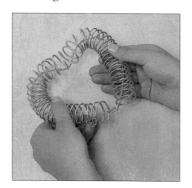

MIRRORED KEEPSAKE BOX

This mirror-decorated trinket box is an original idea for storing jewelry or other small objects. To break the mirror into fragments, put it between sheets of newspaper and hit it with a hammer.

YOU WILL NEED

MATERIALS
section of poster tube
cardboard
masking tape
white glue
newspaper
4 marbles
wallpaper paste
epoxy glue
chemical metal filler (car-body repair filler)
mirror fragments
white acrylic primer
selection of gouache paints
glossy varnish
gold enamel paint

EQUIPMENT
scissors
pencil
pair of compasses
small and fine paintbrushes
paint-mixing containers

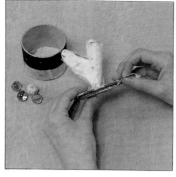

1 Draw around the tube end on cardboard, cut out and tape to the tube. Cut out a slightly larger lid and another circle ½ in less in diameter. Glue together. Bend a roll of newspaper into a heart. Tape to the lid. Cover the marbles with tape.

2 Cover the box, lid and marbles with several layers of newspaper, soaked in wallpaper paste. When dry, glue the marbles to the box base with epoxy glue. Mix up the filler, spread it on the lid, and carefully push in the mirror fragments.

3 Paint the box, not the mirror pieces, with white glue. When dry, prime the box. Paint the design with gouache.

4 Coat with several layers of glossy varnish, and let dry. Add detail in gold enamel.

TEMPLATES

To enlarge the templates to the correct size, either use a grid system or a photocopier. For the grid system, trace the template and draw a grid of evenly spaced squares over your tracing. To scale up, draw a larger grid on to another piece of paper. Copy the outline on to the second grid by taking each square individually and drawing the relevant part of the outline in the larger square. For tracing templates you will need tracing paper, a pencil, paper, and scissors.

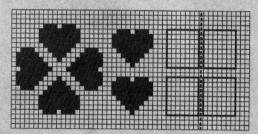

Shaker-style Towel, alphabet chart p34 (enlarge to 220% for actual size)

Decoupaged Valentine's Box p36; Romantic Gift Wrap p38; Embroidered Baby Suit p22

Shaker-style Towel, heart design chart p34 (enlarge to 220% for actual size)

Bridal Heart p50 (enlarge to 330% for actual size)

Heart-shaped Wooden Dish p32 (enlarge to 400% for actual size)

Winged Heart p27
(enlarge to 200% for actual size)

Metallic Embroidered Jewelry p52
(enlarge to 250% for actual size)

Heartfelt Cradle Quilt p16
(enlarge to 200% for actual size)

Hand-painted Wooden Box p20

King of Hearts Mirror p41
(enlarge to 350% for actual size)

Hearts on the Wing Mobile p43
(enlarge to 250% for actual size)

Love Bug p48
(enlarge to 200% for actual size)

Folk-art Picture Frames p46

ACKNOWLEDGEMENTS

The author and publishers would like to thank the following people for designing the projects in this book:

Ofer Acoo

King of Hearts Mirror p41;
Love Bug p48

Amanda Blunden

Love-hearts Wall Plaque p24

Penny Boylan

Cookie Hearts and Hands p29;
Folk-art Picture Frames p46

Louise Brownlow

Hand-painted Wooden Box p20;
Metallic Emboidered Jewelry p52

Lucinda Ganderton

Heartfelt Cradle Quilt p16;
Winged Heart p27;
Shaker-style Towel p34;
Bridal Heart p50

Andrew Gillmore

Love and Kisses Soap Dish p12;
Heart-shaped Trivet p56

Jill Hancock

Heart-shaped Wooden Dish p32

Terence Moore
Moores Design

Heart and Flowers p14

Kim Rowley

Hearts on the Wing Mobile p43;
Mirrored Keepsake Box p58

Kelie-Marie Townsend

Embroidered Baby Suit p22

Josephine Whitfield

Decoupaged Valentine's Box p36;
Romantic Gift Wrap p38